This Book Belongs to:

A NEW BURLINGTON BOOK
The Old Brewery
6 Blundell Street
London N7 9BH

Consultant: Fiona Moss, RE Adviser at RE Today Services
Editor: Cathy Jones
Designer: Chris Fraser
Editorial Assistant: Tasha Percy
Design Manager: Anna Lubecka

First published in the United States by
Part of The Quarto Group
QEB Publishing
6 Orchard
Lake Forest, CA 92630

www.qed-publishing.co.uk

A CIP record for this book is available from the Library of Congress.

ISBN 978 1 60992 570 3

Printed in China

The Birth of Jesus

Written by
Katherine Sully

Illustrated by
Simona Sanfilippo

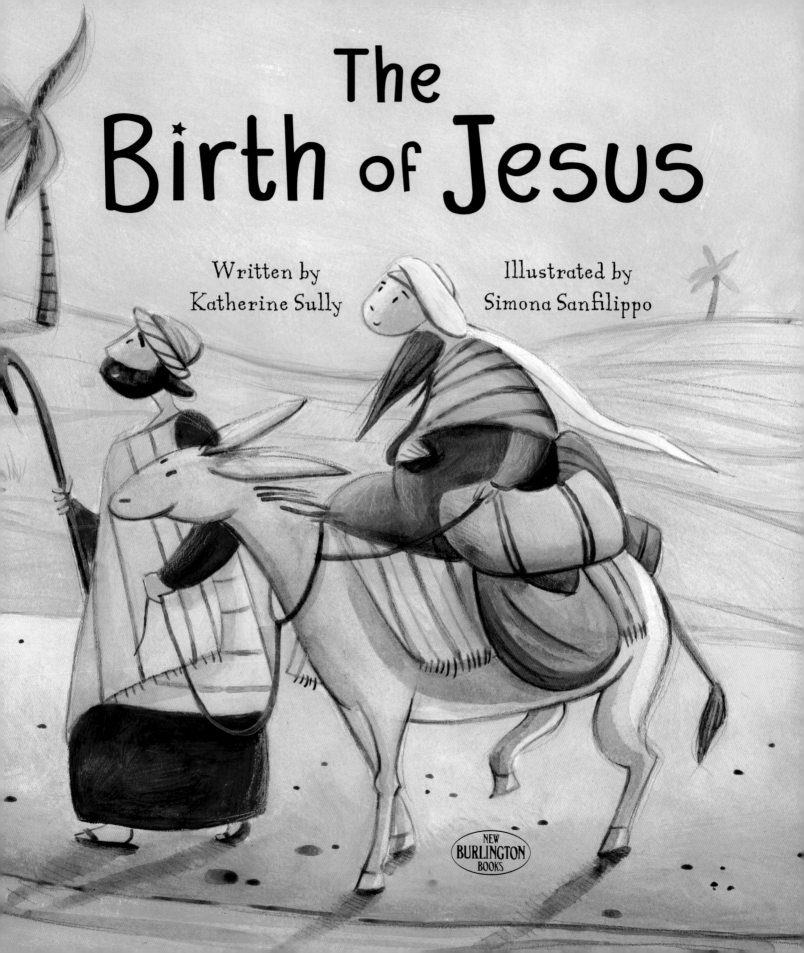

NEW BURLINGTON BOOKS

Long ago, in the town of
Nazareth, lived a young
woman called Mary.
One day, Mary had a shock
—she saw an angel.

The angel Gabriel said,
"Don't be afraid,
I bring you good news
about Christ our Lord,
the king of the Jews."

"God is going to bless you with a baby,"
said Gabriel. "His name will be Jesus."

"I will do as God asks," said Mary.

Now, Mary was engaged to marry Joseph, the carpenter. What would he think about Mary having a baby?

Joseph was upset. But then, one night, he had a dream. In his dream an angel told him all about Mary's baby coming from God.

"You will name the baby Jesus," said the angel.
When Joseph woke up, he understood.

So Joseph and Mary were married.

At this time, everyone had to be counted so that they could pay taxes. Mary and Joseph had to go to Joseph's home town to be counted.

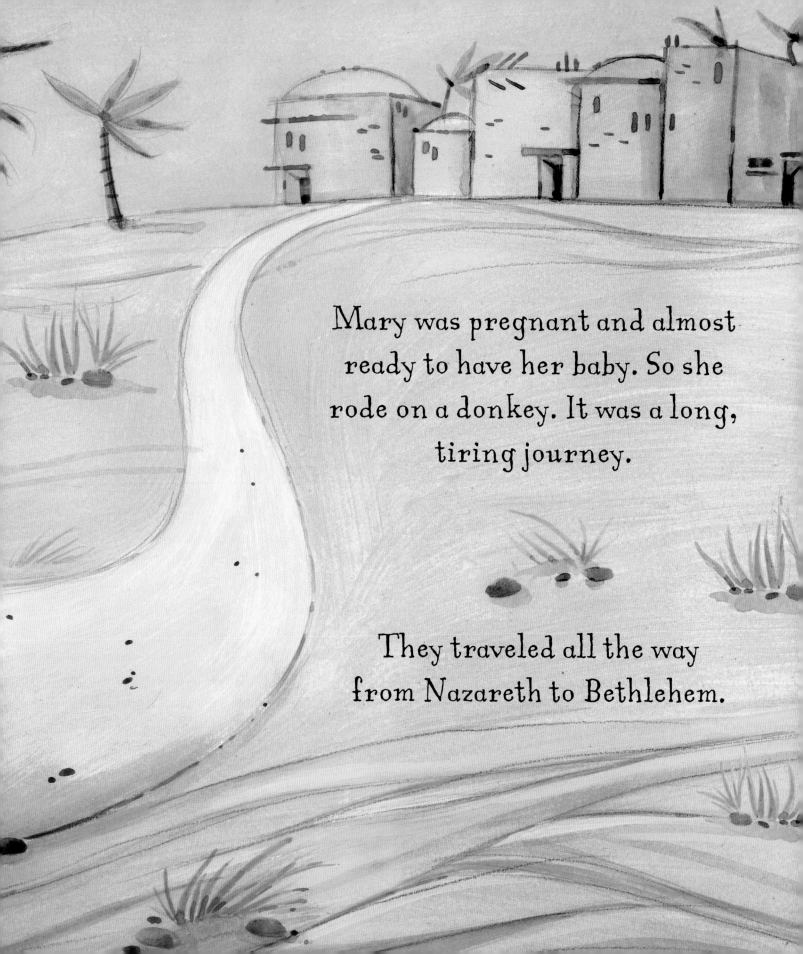

Mary was pregnant and almost ready to have her baby. So she rode on a donkey. It was a long, tiring journey.

They traveled all the way from Nazareth to Bethlehem.

When, at last, Mary and Joseph arrived in Bethlehem, the streets were crowded.

There was no room left at the inn.

What could they do?
Where could they stay?

Joseph found a stable and
Mary settled down in the straw.

That night, baby Jesus was born in the stable.
Mary rocked the baby in her arms.

Then she wrapped him in blankets and laid him gently in a manger of hay.

Moo!

Hee-haw!

The same night, some shepherds
were looking after their sheep.

Baa!

Suddenly, they were afraid.
A crowd of singing angels appeared in the sky.

Baa!

"Don't be afraid,
I bring you good news
about Christ our Lord,
the king of the Jews,"
sang an angel.
"You will find him in a manger."

Baa!

Baa!

Baa!

The shepherds hurried to Bethlehem to see if it was true.

And it was true! They found baby Jesus lying in a manger.

The shepherds thanked God and went
to tell everyone their story.

Far from Bethlehem, three wise men from the east saw a bright star in the night sky.

The star was a sign
—a new king of the
Jews had been born.

They set off on a long
journey to Jerusalem
to see King Herod.
He would know all about it!

"Where is the new king?" the wise men asked King Herod.

King Herod knew nothing about it! He asked his advisers where this new king had been born.

"In Bethlehem, so it is told," they said.
So King Herod sent the wise men to Bethlehem.

"Tell me when you find him," said King Herod.
He didn't want anyone else to be king.

The three wise men followed the star to Bethlehem until it shone above a house.

The wise men found Mary and Jesus inside the house.

They bowed down and gave him gifts of gold, frankincense, and myrrh.

In a dream, the wise men were warned not to tell King Herod where Jesus lived. So they went straight home.

Joseph took Mary and baby Jesus to Egypt, where they were safe from King Herod.

Next Steps

Look back through the book to find more to talk about and join in with.

★ Copy the actions. Do the actions with the characters—rock the baby Jesus in your arms; bow down; follow the star.

★ Join in with the rhyme. Pause to encourage joining in with,
"Don't be afraid, I bring you good news
About Christ our Lord, the king of the Jews."

★ Count in threes. Count three sheep, three hens, three shepherds, three wise men.

★ Name the colors. What colors are the angels wearing? Look back to spot the colors on other pages.

★ All shapes and sizes. Describe the gifts that the wise men bring.

★ Listen to the noisy animals in the stable. When you see the word on the page, point and make the sound—Moo! Baa! Cluck! Hee-haw! Neigh!

Now that you've read the story . . . what do you remember?

★ Who told Mary that she was going to have a baby?
★ What name was Mary told to give the baby?
★ Who was Joseph?
★ Where was Jesus born?
★ How were the shepherds told about Jesus?
★ How did the wise men find Jesus?

What does the story tell us?
God sent us the baby Jesus to be Christ our Lord.